Deep Breaths Darling

Ashaelah Woods

Presentation by *BookLeaf Publishing*

Web: www.bookleafpub.com

E-mail: info@bookleafpub.com

ISBN: 9789358314243

First edition 2023

DEDICATION

To everyone who thinks they walk through life alone.

ACKNOWLEDGEMENT

My favourite thing about writing is that I can express myself. I wouldn't be able to do this without the encouragement from the people around me.

To my family. Thank you all for encouraging me to be the best person I can be. Your support means the world to me!

Special thanks to my mum. Who constantly encouraged me to live out my dreams, even when it seemed impossible.

To my dad who encouraged me to try my best at everything.

To my sisters Aaliyah, Tanesha and Makenna. For always making me smile and giving me inspiration everyday.

To my dog, Gucci, for listening to me rant on about everything.

An enormous thanks to Book Leaf Publishing for giving me the opportunity to publish my poetry.

PREFACE

This book was made to give people something to relate to. Each poem tells a story and speaks to the emotions that someone may have. This books soul purpose is to ensure everyone understands they are not alone.

Angel on Earth

My hands let go but I still hold on,
I still hum the lyrics to this never ending song,
my mind adapted to you not being here,
but that doesn't stop my eyes from shedding a
tear.

I hope where you are will make you happy,
because here it seems like everyone is sappy.

You have opened a new world I need to explore,
even if it was too early for me to open that door.

You make butterflys fly higher with every
memory,
I guess remembering is my remedy.

You make flowers grow taller by the stem,
I get thoughts of you because we used to eat
them.

You were picked too soon!
I had to let go,
I was embarrassed to let my feelings show,
I didn't know what time was worth,
but I was blessed to have met an angel on earth.

In front of everyone I try to keep strong,
but hiding my emotions is completely wrong,
I need to express how I feel,
I shouldn't keep my emotions concealed.

My hands let go but my heart holds on,
I still sing the lyrics to this sad song,
my mind still adapts to you not being here,
and my eyes witness thunderstorms,
not just a single tear.

My Friend ED

I was bullied at school and depressed at home.
I constantly felt alone.

I was called mean names about my weight, how
I spoke and can't stand straight.
That's when ED came around,
said he'd help me lose every pound.

ED told me I would be alright,
all I had to do was fight.
Change myself overnight,
that'll show them, right?

Taught me how to eat and how to weigh,
it wasn't good enough every day.
Explained how to fast and it was tough,
ED was sometimes really rough.

Instructed that I should eat my food and vomit
after,
that will stop my bullies laughter.
When I thought I was done,
ED reminded me that I've just begun.

I started to feel certain things.
Everything changed, even my feelings.
I felt exhausted and nauseous,
I was always thirsty and wasn't cautious.

Bones would show and skin will sink.
Family didn't recognise me, which drew the
link.
ED wasn't my friend after all,
they decided to give the doctor a call.

Confession of Depression

Sorrow is a place the mind goes when the heart
is numb.
It seeps into everything and everyone.

Depression closes in and the world becomes
dark.
Nothing seems to light a spark.

Conversations are miserable and interactions are
clear.
There isn't one person you want to be near.

Loneliness seeps in and you're on your own.
Doesn't matter if you're in public or your home.

Play pretend and fake it all.
No one ever notices the fall.

When you reach the ground nobody picks you
up.
Pretending begins to feel tough.

Reality begins to become clear.
You think the world is better without you here.

You reach the end and had enough.
Say your goodbyes and wish everyone good
luck.

Notice The Signs

She's smiling but her eyes are black and blue,
face expression shifting to.

Her fear shown when she flinches.
I touch her arm,
to give her comfort.
She brushes me off,
acts like it doesn't hurt.
I know it does.

You don't want to blame him,
you claim him,
to be the one you love.
Say he never raised his hand.
He isn't a man,
he's the villain!

Your words speak lies,
your eyes tell the truth.
How can you let him hurt you?
Pay attention and listen clear,
everybody wants to help you here.

Get out before it's gone too far.
Be an example for your daughter.

Your so blind you can't even see,
that you're wrapped around his finger like a vine
on a tree.

You don't want to throw blame,
you'd rather your children feel ashamed.

When he ask for forgiveness don't let it happen,
because then it will turn into a pattern.

I'd Be Your Friend

I cant tell you how much you help me.
You drew a line and I followed,
I am the tail to your being.
you showed me everything.

I listened to your advice,
learn from your mistakes.
I'm so glad we're on the same team,
and turning the same page.

You are a shoulder for me to lean on,
and my tissue for my tears.
I don't know how to repay you.
How do I even thank you,
for helping me conquer all my fears?

The dark corners you pull me out of,
and the sunlight you bring my way.
The happiness you give me,
the memories we make.

You are a blessing from the beginning,
And I'll have you till the end.
So grateful your my family,
but even if u weren't i'd still be your friend.

Precious Time

Life changes at the drop of a hat.
One minute your looking forward,
the next your looking back.

People change and people go.
The ones that stick with you,
are the ones you keep close.

Relationships evolve or disappear.
Today your your happy,
tomorrow your in tears.

Meaning changes over time.
What once was nothing,
might be worth something.

Bridges burn.
Roads close.
Pathways cross.
Relationship grow,
but some are lost.

Time means everything,
but also means nothing.
Make the most of it,

so it's worth something.

My Weeping Willow

In the sunshine,
we had the best time.
Our happiness grew when flowers bloomed.
Shadows loomed.
The smiles make our faces glow.
My weeping willow.

It seemed slow but it went so quick.
Grew so fast time split.
When tears show you grow.
My weeping willow.

We appeared beautiful in the midst of a storm.
The feeling of doubt was born.
Branches broke when we spoke.
Lost feelings, hope and our flow.
My weeping willow.

The beginning was full of butterflies.
The storm began we weren't so wise.
Started in spring,
Fell apart in the snow.
My weeping willow.

30 feet with broken branches.

Piles of leaves and all of these memories,
under my weeping willow.

What Am I Doing Here

I wake up and cannot wait for the day to end.
What has life become?
Where is all my friends?

My inner child screams inside.
When conflict hits there's nowhere to hide.
I'm exhausted of exhaustion and can't decide,
if I'm happy now or out of my mind.

I've lost my path,
what's down this road?
My thoughts so loud my head explodes.

I wouldn't have anticipated or ever known,
that adulthood makes you feel so alone.

There's No Place Like Home

Sunset hits and we're on our way home.
Music pumping loud.
Sunshine dying behind the clouds.
Saying goodbye to the city today,
but I'm not alone when I say,
there's no place like home.

Cold air hits my face.
The sun begins to get replaced.
The moon is out.
The stars start to show.
There's no place like home.

The mountains shadows casted on the car.
I know now that homes not far.
The country air smells so fresh.
Watching the wild animals roam.
There's is no place like home.

The yellow crain begins to appear,
that's how you know your here.
See the twinkle of the lights and you know,
there's no place like home.

I Don't Want To Miss You

I'm the person you turn to when you feel alone.
I'm the person you run to when you're running
from home.
I'm the one who will stay up to calm your
nerves,
fix your burdens,
and help you feel better not worse.

I'm the person who listens to your cries.
I'm the person that picks you up when you're
down.
When everybody else is not around,
I'll get you home safe and sound.

I'll be with you through it all.
All you have to do is knock on my door,
give me a call,
and I'll be there.
Im the one who prays,
that you will have better days.

I'm the person who takes on your burdens.
I'm the one who's hurting if you're uncertain,
about whether you should be.
I will make you see how much you mean to me.

I'll try to fix you,
so I don't have to miss you.

Blessing at Birth

You were brought to us out of the blue,
in a world where everything felt doomed.
The little sparkle that lit our eyes,
and now I sing you lullabies.

You came about in the darkest days.
God surprised us in the greatest way.
You pulled us out of depression,
and changed our facial expressions.

Sprinkling happiness with every stumble.
You keep us humble.
The world is brighter with you in it.
Without you it would have been easier to quit.

You don't realise how much you saved me,
even though you're just a little baby.
When you were born my heart strings were
tugged.
Please understand you're truely loved.

For The Wisher

I wished upon a star one night,
and thought I saw a light.
The little sparkle lit up my eye,
it shined so bright it made me cry.

My lips began to smile but started to twist,
I felt as if I shouldn't have wished.
It gave me such a fright,
but I knew it would be alright.

With that little sparkle there was hope,
that it might change my life.
So I closed my eyes,
laid down to sleep,
and wished the world goodnight.

Your Everywhere

Yesterday I turned around and saw your face.
My emotions went all over the place.

I can't live in a world where you're not here.
How does someone just disappear.

What I'd give if I had a choice,
to hear you speak and listen to your voice.

I remember a day when you were near,
and I stop myself from shedding a tear.

Death has become one of my biggest fears.
Even thought everything about it is unclear.

Thank you for everything you have done.
You helped me turn into the person I've become.

Who Have I Become

I wake up and cannot wait for the day to end.
What has life become?
Where is all my friends?

My inner child screams inside.
When conflict hits there's nowhere to hide.
I'm exhausted of exhaustion and can't decide,
If I'm happy now or out of my mind.

I've lost my path,
what's down this road?
My thoughts so loud my head explodes.

I wouldn't have anticipated or ever known,
That adulthood makes you feel so alone.

Loneliness Is A Disease

The world is overcome by lonely people.
That's a disease that is fatal.
I don't want to walk through life alone.
I wouldn't know where to roam.

Everything is new to me.
It would be the first time I get to breathe.
I haven't done anything wrong,
is that a problem?

You need experience to know how to live.
I haven't done anything different, to when I was
a kid.
I tell everyone I'm fine,
I want to scream and shout at the same time.

Has the string been to tight for error?
Have I missed out on my most important era?
I don't want my life to turn into a disaster,
so all these thought are turned into laughter.

One day I might be a lonely person.
I know it will be my fault for carrying this
burden.
I wish I never tried so hard to impress you.

I can't place blame, you never knew.

Twin Flame

Show me your insecurities and I'll show you
mine.
Mirror me like you do all the time.
We're exact opposites but also the same.
Sometimes the only difference is our names.

Tell me my fears,
I'll tell you yours.
Our heart bond is eternal.
You're forever in my thoughts.

We reunited the day you were born.
We took the world by storm.
Our souls were split into two,
until I met you.

We're the missing pieces to each other,
that's why we need one another.
You force me to confront my biggest fears,
and your always there to catch my tears.

Everything you do is with a good heart.
I know we aren't meant to be apart.
Even when we fight there's no one else to
blame.

I guess I'm lucky to have met my twin flame.

Sweet Mother of Mine

Without you the darkness will creep in,
the world will become dull,
and coldness will feel the air.
Because right now your warmth is everywhere.

I don't think I'll smile again.
Your not just my mother,
but my best friend.
So if you weren't here I think I'd disappear as
well.

With everything you've been through,
how do you stay so strong?
How do you keep on the path you stroll on?
My inspiration and my idol.
I'll take notes off you like I do with the bible.

Thank for the lessons and the time you put in,
to teach me everything.
I appreciate you so much.
Every breakfast, dinner and lunch.

You made me who I am today.
You're as golden as a sunshine ray.
Thanks for the sleepless nights and joyful times.

You didn't meet me at the top you were there
during the climb.
Sweet mother of mine.

Care for Earth

Count the drops of salt water on your hand.
Feel your toes sink in the sand.
Look around at this beautiful land,
and wonder what is gods plan.

Hear the patter of the rain on your umbrella.
Appreciate that we're all together.
Press the button to let it down.
Feel your hair go wet as you stumble around.

Connect the stars.
Find the constellation.
stare at gods creations,
like I have all the patience.

Stare at the moon with me.
Look at the same star.
The sky seems close to us.
Makes me feel like you're not that far.

Squint at the sun,
and make shapes in the clouds.
Pick up a dandelion,
and count the petals out loudly.

Feel the wind in your hair.
Watch leaves fall everywhere.
This earth will make you stop and stare.
There's nothing that can compare.
So wake up and be aware,
we need to treat it with every ounce of care.

Anxiety

My brain is full of everything.
It's hard for me to focus.
I try to stay calm,
but my heart beats so fast.

My breathing is heavier.
I'm sweating in the palms.
My face is white,
and my throat is dry.

Look me in the eyes,
and tell me it's okay.
Yesterday I was worried,
but today I am afraid.

I can feel it creeping in.
I try to contain myself.
I feel a weight on my shoulders.
Assumed it would get better,
as I got older.

Trembling in my feet.
Stutter as I speak.
Start to feel depressed,
from this emotional distress.

This continues weekly.
It's weakening me.
It happens every time I'm in society.
I guess that's the case,
when you struggle with anxiety.

Perfect Gift From God

I reached out to god with my prayers.
He sent me a dog with so many layers.
The perfect gift from our Heavenly Father.
To send a dog that would create so much
laughter.

The perfect piece to our puzzle,
in a time where the world was a struggle.
You lift your nose to my ear and nuzzle.
Lick my chin and give me a cuddle.

The way your tail wags when your excited,
makes me feel so delighted.
Dress you up for a fashion show.
You are my yellow.

You're the reason for the smile on my face.
Nothing could ever take your place.
The way you lay your head on my heart.
The happiness in you, when you bark.

Your a match,
You lit my spark.
Showed me a world of light,
not dark.

You became an explorer,
when you met Dora.
My heart hurt,
when you were mourning for her.

All these years,
we collected each others tears.
You listened to my fears,
with your perfect set of ears.

Watch you get old,
as you watch me grow.
Together our ages show.
God does wonderful things up above.
To send me you and all your love.

www.ingramcontent.com/pod-product-compliance
Lightning Source LLC
LaVergne TN
LVHW010927200726
843509LV00013B/2107